Let's Fly

HELICOPTERS

by Wendy Hinote Lanier

FOCUS READERS

www.focusreaders.com

Focus Readers is distributed by North Star Editions:
sales@northstareditions.com | 888-417-0195

Produced for Focus Readers by Red Line Editorial.

Photographs ©: Makushin Alexey/Shutterstock Images, cover, 1; Olga Steckel/Shutterstock Images, 4–5; ID1974/Shutterstock Images, 7; Harris & Ewing/Harris & Ewing Collection/Library of Congress, 8–9; USCG Photo #232-8/US Coast Guard, 11; Ivan Cholakov/Shutterstock Images, 12, 18, 29; plantic/Shutterstock Images, 14–15; Nattapon B/Shutterstock Images, 17; Guy Cowdry/Shutterstock Images, 20–21; max blain/Shutterstock Images, 22–23; Tom Reichner/Shutterstock Images, 24; VanderWolf Images/Shutterstock Images, 27

Library of Congress Cataloging-in-Publication Data
Names: Lanier, Wendy Hinote, author.
Title: Helicopters / by Wendy Hinote Lanier.
Description: Lake Elmo, MN : Focus Readers, [2019] | Series: Let's fly | Audience: Grades 4 to 6. | Includes bibliographical references and index. Identifiers: LCCN 2018030376 (print) | LCCN 2018031763 (ebook) | ISBN 9781641855136 (PDF) | ISBN 9781641854559 (ebook) | ISBN 9781641853392 (hardcover) | ISBN 9781641853972 (paperback)
Subjects: LCSH: Helicopters--Juvenile literature.
Classification: LCC TL716.2 (ebook) | LCC TL716.2 .L37 2019 (print) | DDC 629.133/352--dc23
LC record available at https://lccn.loc.gov/2018030376

Printed in the United States of America
Mankato, MN
October, 2018

About the Author

Wendy Hinote Lanier is a native Texan and former elementary teacher who writes and speaks for children and adults on a variety of topics. She is the author of more than 30 books for children and young adults.

TABLE OF CONTENTS

LIFE FORCE
erlanger

CHAPTER 1

TO THE RESCUE

Sirens blare. A car has spun off the road. The car has crashed into a fence. The driver is hurt. She needs to go to a hospital. There are no towns nearby. But help is on the way.

A medical helicopter lands near an accident.

Another loud noise fills the air. A helicopter flies toward the crash. Its **rotors** make a *thup, thup, thup* sound. The helicopter **hovers** above the car. Then it lands in a field by the road. Unlike an airplane, a helicopter does not need a runway.

FUN FACT

Helicopters are sometimes called choppers. This name comes from the sound their rotors make.

Inside a medical helicopter, there are beds and supplies to care for sick or hurt people.

It can take off and land straight up and down.

The hurt woman is carried inside the helicopter. Then it rises into the air. It takes her to the hospital.

CHAPTER 2

HELICOPTER HISTORY

Before helicopters, people flew in autogiros. Autogiros were invented in the 1920s. They looked like a mix of an airplane and a helicopter. Autogiros had rotors. But their rotors were turned by air.

An autogiro lands in Washington, DC, in the 1930s.

A helicopter's rotors are turned by engines.

The first helicopter was invented in Germany. It was built in 1936. It looked similar to an airplane. But instead of wings, it had rotors. One rotor was on each side. Each rotor had three blades.

FUN FACT

Autogiros were popular in the 1930s. They carried passengers. They delivered mail. One autogiro even explored Antarctica!

The Sikorsky R-4 helicopter inspired many modern designs.

A new kind of helicopter flew in 1939. One rotor was on the top. It had three blades. The other rotor was on the tail. This rotor had two blades. Today's helicopters are based on this design.

The Bell UH-1 was a common US helicopter during the Vietnam War (1955–1975).

The **turbine** engine appeared in the 1950s. This engine made helicopters faster. They could also carry more weight for longer distances.

Many helicopters flew during the Vietnam War (1955–1975). They carried soldiers, supplies, and weapons. Helicopters have not changed much since then. But they have become more common.

USES IN WAR

The Vietnam War is sometimes called the Helicopter War. That is because helicopters did many jobs. They rescued people from dangerous areas. They brought hurt soldiers to hospitals. And they flew over enemy areas to help soldiers spot the other side's troops.

CHAPTER 3

SPINNING BLADES

Helicopters get power from turbine engines. An engine burns fuel to make a rush of hot air. The air spins a turbine. The turning turbine produces power. The **transmission** sends this power to the rotors.

A helicopter's rotors are made of strong, lightweight material.

The rotor mast connects the rotor blades to the transmission. Rotor blades spin very fast. They create lift. This upward force causes the helicopter to rise into the air. Most helicopters have a main rotor and a tail rotor. But some have two main rotors.

FUN FACT

Many helicopters do not have wheels or brakes. Instead, they land on two hollow tubes called skids.

A stabilizer bar sits above the spinning rotor blades.

The engine and rotors make the helicopter shake. So, some helicopters have a stabilizer bar.

PARTS OF A HELICOPTER

A stabilizer bar goes across and above the main rotor blade. The bar reduces the shaking. Less shaking keeps the helicopter steady.

A helicopter's body is called the fuselage. The cockpit is at the front. The tail boom attaches to the back. This part looks like a long tube. It connects the tail rotors to the fuselage.

IN THE AIR

Because of its rotors, a helicopter can move in many ways. The rotors allow the helicopter to take off straight up and down. In the air, the rotors help the helicopter turn. They can also change its **altitude**. They can make it hover, too.

HOW IT WORKS

TILTING AND TURNING

Helicopters can fly forward or backward. They can even fly sideways. Pilots use levers and pedals to steer. Two levers control the main rotors. One lever moves the helicopter up and down. The other lever **tilts** the rotor blades. The helicopter will tilt the same direction. Helicopters can tilt up or down. They can also lean side to side.

Foot pedals control the tail rotors. Pushing one pedal turns the helicopter to the left. To turn right, the pilot pushes the other pedal. Pilots operate the pedals and levers at the same time.

Steering levers are in front of the control panel. Foot pedals are underneath.

VNE 130 KTS WITH POD FITTED
FLIGHTS IN IMC ARE PROHIBITED
EMERGENCY CUT OFF
DQ HFT
ISLAND AIR 02
AIRSPEED
KNOTS
ALT
INSTANTANEOUS VERTICAL SPEED
RADAR ALTITUDE
BUS SHED
BUS XFER

VH-SCO
FIREBIRD
322
Surf Coast
Byron BAY PREMIUM ALE
14

CHAPTER 4

MODERN CHOPPERS

Today, there are many kinds of helicopters. They do various jobs. Some carry heavy loads. They are used for construction work. Others take photos or videos from the air.

A news helicopter films a boat race in Corio Bay, Australia.

Firefighters use helicopters to stop wildfires from spreading.

They gather news and report on traffic.

Helicopters help in emergencies as well. Some help put out fires.

They spray water and chemicals. The spray protects trees and plants from the flames. Other helicopters are used for search and rescue. They fly over **remote** areas. They find people who are hurt or lost. Helicopters also bring hurt people to hospitals.

FUN FACT

A helicopter's blades keep spinning if the engine stops. This gives the pilot time to make a safe landing.

Many helicopters have autopilot. This computer system can fly and steer the helicopter without help from the pilot. **GPS** is also common. It tells the pilot where to go. Other **instruments** tell the pilot what

PART PLANE

The V-22 Osprey is a combination of a helicopter and an airplane. The vehicle takes off and lands like a helicopter. In the air, its two main rotors tip forward. Then it flies like an airplane. This amazing aircraft can fly 315 miles per hour (507 km/h).

A V-22 Osprey's rotors tip forward as it rises into the air.

other aircraft are nearby. They warn the pilot if another aircraft gets too close. This helps the pilot avoid a crash. Inventions such as these help make flying safe.

FOCUS ON

HELICOPTERS

Write your answers on a separate piece of paper.

1. Write a letter to a friend describing the history of helicopters.
2. Would you want to fly a helicopter? Why or why not?
3. When were the first helicopters invented?
   - A. the 1920s
   - B. the 1930s
   - C. the 1950s
4. What would happen if a helicopter's transmission stopped working?
   - A. The rotor blades would not turn.
   - B. The rotor blades would fall off.
   - C. The rotor blades would bend in half.

5. What does **runway** mean in this book?

Unlike an airplane, a helicopter does not need a ***runway****. It can take off and land straight up and down.*

A. a wide, flat road where many cars can drive

B. a narrow path where people can walk

C. a long strip of level ground where airplanes land

6. What does **emergencies** mean in this book?

Helicopters help in ***emergencies*** *as well. Some help put out fires.*

A. loud events where it is hard to hear

B. calm events where people can relax

C. dangerous events where help is needed

Answer key on page 32.

GLOSSARY

altitude
Height above the ground.

GPS
A navigation system that uses satellites to figure out location.

hovers
Stays in one place in the air.

instruments
Devices used for collecting information, navigating, or controlling the movement of an aircraft.

remote
Far away from cities or other places.

rotors
Horizontal sets of spinning blades that provide lift.

tilts
Leans or tips in one direction.

transmission
A set of gears that convert power from a helicopter's engine to power that can turn its rotors.

turbine
A wheel that is turned by air, water, or steam and used to produce power.

TO LEARN MORE

BOOKS

Confalone, Chelsea, and Nick Confalone. *Helicopters*. New York: Grosset & Dunlap, 2015.

Cooke, Tim. *A Timeline of Helicopters*. North Mankato, MN: Capstone Press, 2018.

Fretland VanVoorst, Jenny. *Helicopters*. Minneapolis: Jump!, 2018.

NOTE TO EDUCATORS

Visit **www.focusreaders.com** to find lesson plans, activities, links, and other resources related to this title.

INDEX

Answer Key: 1. Answers will vary; **2.** Answers will vary; **3.** B; **4.** A; **5.** C; **6.** C